OPPOSITES

All Around Me!

HOT and COLD

A Crabtree Roots Book

AMY CULLIFORD

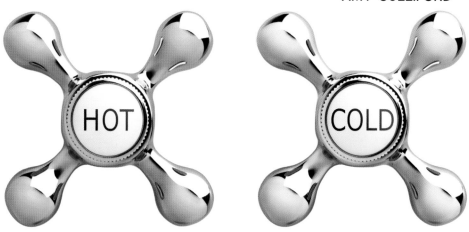

CRABTREE
Publishing Company
www.crabtreebooks.com

School-to-Home Support for Caregivers and Teachers

This book helps children grow by letting them practice reading. Here are a few guiding questions to help the reader with building his or her comprehension skills. Possible answers appear here in red.

Before Reading:

• What do I think this book is about?
- *This book is about hot things and cold things.*
- *This book is about what cold things and hot things look like.*

• What do I want to learn about this topic?
- *I want to learn what cold things look like.*
- *I want to learn why some things are hot and some are cold.*

During Reading:

• I wonder why...
- *I wonder why fire is hot.*
- *I wonder why ice is cold.*

• What have I learned so far?
- *I have learned that food can be hot or cold.*
- *I have learned that hot and cold are opposites.*

After Reading:

• What details did I learn about this topic?
- *I have learned that drinks can be hot or cold.*
- *I have learned that ice and fire are opposites.*

• Read the book again and look for the vocabulary words.
- *I see the word **campfire** on page 5 and the word **drink** on page 8. The other vocabulary words are found on page 14.*

What is **hot**, and
what is **cold**?

A **campfire** is hot.

Ice is cold.

This **drink** is hot.

This drink is cold.

This **breakfast** is hot.

This breakfast is cold.

13

Word List

Sight Words

a	is	what
and	this	

Words to Know

breakfast	campfire	cold

drink	hot	ice

30 Words

What is **hot**, and what is **cold**?

A **campfire** is hot.

Ice is cold.

This **drink** is hot.

This drink is cold.

This **breakfast** is hot.

This breakfast is cold.

OPPOSITES

All Around Me!

HOT and COLD

Written by: Amy Culliford
Designed by: Rhea Wallace
Series Development: James Earley
Proofreader: Ellen Rodger
Educational Consultant: Marie Lemke M.Ed.

Photographs:
Shutterstock: Michael C Gray: cover (left); GrigoryL:
cover (right); ifong: p. 1; Volodymyr Plysiuk: p. 3,
14; Claudiu Maxim: p. 4, 14; Valentyn Volov: p. 6,
14; Subbotina Anna: p. 8, 14; Joshua Resnick: p. 9;
Tatiana Chekryzhova: p. 10, 14; chris_tina: p. 13

Library and Archives Canada Cataloguing in Publication

Title: Hot and cold / Amy Culliford.
Names: Culliford, Amy, 1992- author.
  Description: Series statement: Opposites all around me! | "A Crabtree
  roots book".
Identifiers: Canadiana (print) 20210159391 | Canadiana (ebook)
  20210159413 | ISBN 9781427140197
  (hardcover) | ISBN 9781427140258 (softcover) | ISBN 9781427133564
  (HTML) | ISBN 9781427140319
  (read-along ebook) | ISBN 9781427134165 (EPUB)
Subjects: LCSH: Heat—Juvenile literature. | LCSH: Cold—Juvenile literature.
  | LCSH: Polarity— Juvenile literature. | LCSH: English language—Synonyms
  and antonyms— Juvenile literature.
Classification: LCC QC256 .C85 2021 | DDC j536/.5—dc23

Library of Congress Cataloging-in-Publication Data

Names: Culliford, Amy, 1992- author.
Title: Hot and cold / Amy Culliford.
Description: New York, NY : Crabtree Publishing Company, [2022] | Series:
  Opposites all around me - a Crabtree roots book | Includes index. |
  Audience: Ages 4-6 | Audience: Grades K-1
Identifiers: LCCN 2021010771 (print) | LCCN 2021010772 (ebook) | ISBN
  9781427140197 (hardcover) | ISBN 9781427140258 (paperback) | ISBN
  9781427133564 (ebook) | ISBN 9781427134165 (epub) | ISBN 9781427140319
  (read along)
Subjects: LCSH: Heat--Juvenile literature. | Cold--Juvenile literature. |
  Polarity--Juvenile literature. | English language--Synonyms and
  antonyms--Juvenile literature.
Classification: LCC QC256 .C85 2022 (print) | LCC QC256 (ebook) | DDC
  536--dc23
LC record available at https://lccn.loc.gov/2021010771
LC ebook record available at https://lccn.loc.gov/2021010772

Crabtree Publishing Company

www.crabtreebooks.com   1-800-387-7650

Published in the United States
Crabtree Publishing
347 Fifth Avenue, Suite 1402-145
New York, NY, 10016

Published in Canada
Crabtree Publishing
616 Welland Ave.
St. Catharines, Ontario L2M 5V6